Handmade
Watercolour
Greetings Cards

I dedicate this book to Roz Dace
who had such confidence in me.

Handmade
Watercolour
Greetings Cards

Jane Greenwood

SEARCH PRESS

First published in Great Britain 2004

Search Press Limited
Wellwood, North Farm Road,
Tunbridge Wells, Kent TN2 3DR

Text copyright © Jane Greenwood
Photographs by Roddy Paine Photographic Studios
Photographs and design copyright © Search Press Ltd. 2004

ISBN 1 903975 78 6

Readers are permitted to reproduce any of the cards or
patterns in this book for their own use, or for the purposes of
selling for charity, free of charge and without the prior
permission of the Publishers. Any use of the material in this
book for commercial purposes is not permitted without the
prior permission of the Publishers.

The Publishers and author can accept no responsibility for any
consequences arising from the information, advice or
instructions given in this publication.

If you have difficulty obtaining any of the equipment or
materials mentioned in this book, please visit our website at
www.searchpress.com.

Alternatively, you can write to the Publishers, at the address
above, for a current list of stockists, including firms which
operate a mail-order service.

Publishers' note

All the step-by-step photographs in this book feature the
author, Jane Greenwood, demonstrating how to make
handmade greetings cards. No models have been used.

Manufactured by Classic Scan Pte Ltd, Singapore
Printed in Malaysia by Times Offset (M) Sdn, Bhd

*My very grateful thanks to Natasha who
helped me with all the text; to
Caroline Coate whose watercolours on the
wall gave me so much inspiration; to my
wonderful editor Sophie Kersey; Juan who
did the art direction and Roddy who took
the pictures.*

Cover
Daisy
*The very simplest flower, a daisy, can be painted from
memory. Imposing the brilliant white petals on a strong
background of cobalt blue creates a striking card.*

Page 1
Chicken on the Run
*The spattering technique adds action to a painting, and the
addition of a real feather to the card creates humour. The
bright orange card sets off this lively scene perfectly.*

Page 3
Morning Glory
*The wax resist technique is very immediate when you want to
make a spontaneous colour sketch of a flower like this. Keep a
white candle stub in your watercolour box for highlighting or
saving lighter areas.*

Page 5
Still Life: Shells
*The things you love around you are the things you will paint
best. These simple organic shapes with their gentle colours
delight me endlessly, and it is a pleasure to paint them as
they keep still! The plain blue background turns this painting
into an effective card.*

Contents

Introduction

In my thirty years as an illustrator I have always kept watercolour painting as a valued hobby. For my work I use inks for their permanence. The joy of watercolour, by contrast, is its spontaneity: rather than planning rigidly how you are going to paint a subject, you can let accidents and surprises happen – like the little fish in the aqueous painting at bottom left. Here, washes used with salt looked like a marine landscape, so I added fish to complete the picture. Surprises like this make ideal artwork for cards.

Many things in this book, such as the daisy on the cover and the seascape are made up. Simple forms with imagined colour schemes can be turned into an effective card by simply cutting them out and mounting them on coloured card with a frame or line border in a complementary colour.

The lemons and the vase of flowers were painted from life, and I have shown how you can add drama and interest to such paintings by adding a striking patterned background to the lemons, traced from a scarf, or looking at the flower arrangement from a different angle.

I have included simple outlines of the subjects which you can trace to give structure to your paintings, but you can also trace animals and birds from books and magazines. Seed catalogues make wonderful reference for flowers.

The decorative items give a fun, three-dimensional effect to the cards and all sorts of interesting bits can be found at craft shops, around the house or on walks.

I do hope this book will inspire card makers who have been discouraged by watercolours due to the impression that they are too difficult. Don't be put off! Following these simple steps, you will quickly get the knack and appreciate their ease and rapidity of use. I hope that the watercolourists who buy this book will also be inspired by the range of ideas shown. Good luck and I hope you enjoy yourselves as much as I did when making the cards for this book.

Jane A Greenwood

Materials

Greetings cards are small in scale, and so I have used very simple materials sold in high street shops, such as paint sets, small pads of watercolour paper and a few brushes, sponges and things from the bathroom cupboard like cotton buds and paper tissues.

Paper

Watercolour paper comes not only in loose sheets but also in many different sized pads and blocks, and in different weights and textures. Some pads are sealed round the edges and some are spiral-bound. It is best to buy these in the heavier weights such as 250–300gsm (90–140lb) so that the paper will not buckle when wet. You do not need to buy anything larger than an A4 format for the paintings, and one sheet of 25 x 27.5cm (9 x 10¾in) watercolour paper for a background card.

Tracing paper also comes in pads, which are easier to use and keep clean and flat than large, unwieldy sheets. You can buy specially made card blanks and card in larger sheets to cut down in all colours from art and craft shops. Make sure you buy card that is stiff enough on which to mount the watercolour paintings.

Sketchpads are useful for planning the design of your card. You do not need to buy a professional one – a children's sketchpad is fine.

Card blanks, card, paper, self-adhesive memo notes, tracing paper, watercolour pads and blocks and a sketchpad.

Painting materials

The little watercolour paint sets I use were perfect for this book. They contain all the primary colours and the few secondary colours that you will ever need and they even come with a palette and brush!

I have used a few good quality watercolour paints in tubes for mixing up larger washes. The Artists' colours are more expensive but have more brilliance and transparency. I have used Prussian blue, viridian, cadmium yellow, cadmium red, burnt umber, yellow ochre, cerulean blue, alizarin crimson, cadmium lemon, lemon yellow and ultramarine blue for the cards shown in this book. White gouache is useful for spattering as it is opaque, and it can also be used for painting lines around paintings on coloured mounting card.

You'll need one large palette for mixing washes and a small selection of brushes. I tend to use a very large brush, a no. 12 round with a good point for most work; a couple of smaller rounds, numbers 6, 4 and 2 for the detail and a rigger, so called because it is used for painting the rigging on ships, for very fine detail. The flat brushes are useful for washes: I used a long broad one and a smaller one.

A toothbrush is used to spatter paint and kitchen salt to create lovely cracked effects in a wet wash. A candle can be used to create wax resist, cotton buds for mopping up little mistakes and paper tissues for bigger spillages! A natural sponge can be used to apply or lift off paint. I always use a sawn-off plastic water bottle for my water as the base is sturdy and broad.

Watercolour tubes and paint sets, white gouache, a water container, palette, brushes, candle, cotton buds, toothbrush, sponge, paper tissue and kitchen salt.

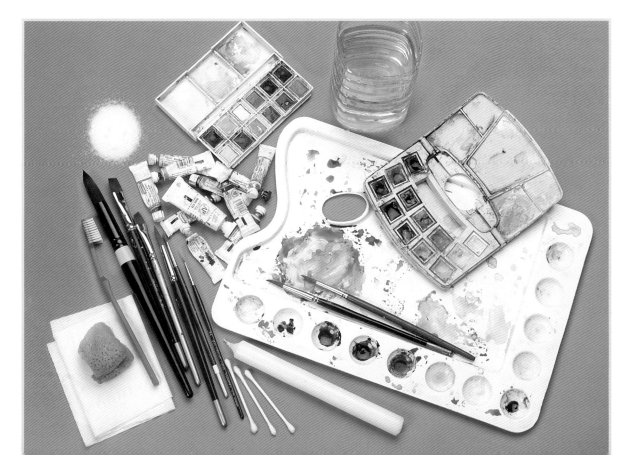

Other materials

I used a handful of disposable push-up pencils for a nice fine line, a fatter, soft-leaded push-up pencil for sketching and tracing, and those lovely metallic gold gel pens for drawing a border round a card or for writing inside a dark-coloured card.

I always use a good cutting mat to cut the card as it has nice straight lines as guides and is kind to the knife blades. I usually use a heavy-duty craft knife to cut the card and a smaller scalpel for scoring paper or cutting out holes to introduce embellishments in a card.

For mounting card I used very thin double-sided tape, a tube of all-purpose glue and a can of spray mount which can be used with thin, smooth paper. You can use 3D foam squares when you want a raised effect – see the snails on page 41. You will need two different pairs of scissors for cutting the sticky tape and the feathers and a putty eraser to clean up smudges of pencil when working with tracings. The little set squares and rulers can be bought in any supermarket; they are intended for children but are perfect for these little jobs.

Masking fluid is essential for blocking out shapes that you want to stay white while you are painting a darker background.

A cutting mat, ruler, craft knives and blades, paper scissors, putty eraser, all-purpose glue, spray mount, 3D foam squares, double-sided tape, set squares, masking fluid, push-up pencils, gold gel pens and nail scissors.

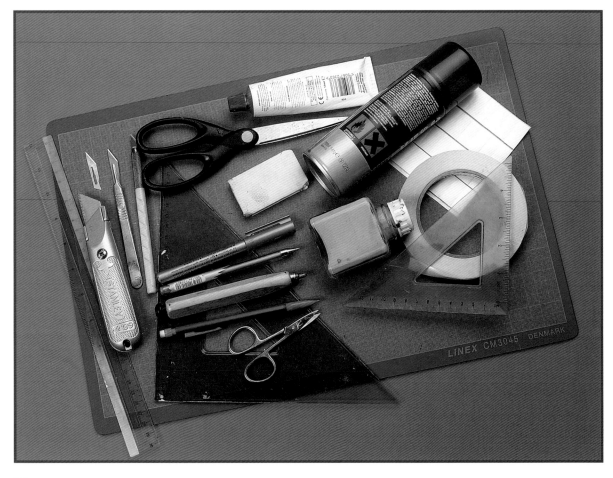

Decorative items

With the enormous range of products now produced for card makers, one is tempted while wandering around a craft shop to think not 'What can I find for that particular project?' but, 'Oh what fun! What can I do with that?' In this way the embellishments provide the springboard to new card ideas.

I have bags containing little strips of coloured card for choosing frames; packets of leaf skeletons and bags of pretty, dyed duck feathers in all colours. Most of my feathers have been collected on visits to country houses with peacocks. The dusky coloured lady peacock feathers are very beautiful, as are guinea fowl and pheasant feathers. Ordinary things found around the house can also be used, such as cotton wool balls for bunny tails and string for a cow's tail.

Cotton wool balls, dyed duck feathers, natural feathers and household string.

Basic techniques

A graduated wash

This is the first thing you learn when getting accustomed to watercolours. A wash is used mostly for backgrounds but can be the subject of a painting, too. In this case we are making a graduated wash to look like a sky.

You will need

Small watercolour pad, 300gsm (140lb)

Brushes: no. 12 and no. 6 round, flat

Watercolours: Prussian blue, viridian, cadmium yellow

White gouache

Toothbrush

Salt

Natural sponge

Masking fluid

White candle

1. Mix Prussian blue with three times as much water. Take the no. 12 brush and brush across the paper in horizontal strokes from the top downwards, adding more water as you reach the bottom. Never go back over the wet paint.

2. Tip the paper to accentuate any effects you desire as the paint spreads into the water.

Spattering

The basic wash looked like a seascape to me, so I added some rocks and sea spray to create a feeling of movement. You can spatter using a paintbrush or a toothbrush.

Tip

Practise both techniques first so that you can control the direction of the spatters.

Load the brush with white gouache and flick the brush diagonally across the paper. Keep the brush at least 7.5cm (3in) from the paper.

A toothbrush can be used if you want the spatters to spread freely over a large area.

12

Wet in wet

This technique involves dropping colours into a wet wash. Surprising effects can occur when colours are mixed in this way and one spreads slowly into the other.

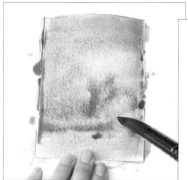

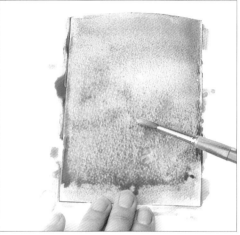

2. Take the smaller brush and drop a mix of cadmium yellow in to the lighter areas of green. Clear water can also be dropped in to lighten the washes.

1. Using the larger brush, paint a wash of Prussian blue. Then load the brush with viridian and drop the green into the blue. Watch the colours spread and mix.

Using salt

While washes are very wet, you can experiment with salt crystals which create unusual patterned effects.

1. While the washes are wet, sprinkle salt on the paper and watch the effects begin as the paint dries.

2. When dry, the salt can be removed using a dry brush.

3. I decided that the salt effects produced during this demonstration looked like a marine landscape, so I lifted out a couple of fish shapes with a clean, dry brush.

Lifting out

Once you have created a graduated wash, you can invent a landscape by lifting out paint to create a cloudy sky or simply by lightening the horizon to suggest the sea. You could also add a field or a beach in this way.

1. Using a small sponge, soaked in water and squeezed out, lift out cloud shapes from the wet wash. Roll the sponge over so that you are using a paint-free area each time.

2. Take a small, flat brush and drag it through the still wet wash two-thirds of the way down the painting, to suggest a horizon.

Masking

You can paint a simple image with masking fluid, either on white paper or on top of a light wash. Then paint a wash over it. When the wash is dry, the masking fluid can be rubbed off with your finger and a startling white image or an area of lighter wash is saved. This can be left as it is, painted in another colour or given form using shadow and tone.

3. When the wash is dry, rub off the masking fluid with a clean finger.

1. Paint a simple shape using masking fluid and an old brush. Wash out the brush immediately.

2. When the masking fluid is dry, wash over the top with Prussian blue. Thin the wash at the bottom of the painting.

Wax resist

A candle or a piece of candle can create a resist over which to paint in watercolour. This is quicker but less precise than using masking fluid.

1. Use a white wax candle to draw a simple design.

2. Apply your wash over the candle wax and the design will appear.

Tip

Direct a strong light on to the paper while using the candle so that you can see what you are drawing.

You can cut out the paintings with fancy-edged scissors or paint a wavy frame around them. Mount them on card in a contrasting colour or tone.

Seascape at Sunset

Try to include three elements in a composition. Here you have the sky, land and a strip of water at low tide. Within these simple elements there are myriad effects you can create. I have divided a sheet of paper into three long, thin sections. The long, vertical format works well with seascapes but it is hard to paint freely in it as it is so narrow. Painting three at the same time helps you to loosen up and if one section doesn't work, another will. The sections measure 6.5cm x 18cm (2½ x 7in) with 1cm (½in) between them.

You will need

Watercolour paper, A4, 300gsm (140lb)

Brushes: no. 6 round brush and rigger

Watercolours: cadmium yellow, cadmium red and burnt umber

Scrap paper and pencil

White card 220 x 240mm (8½ x 9½in)

Craft knife and cutting mat

Set square or ruler

All-purpose glue

Tip

Use a sheet of scrap paper to protect the bottom section of the paintings from drips while working on the top.

1. Take a wash of cadmium yellow and a no. 6 brush. Wash over the tops of your three sections, leave some white paper and then make more streaks of yellow lower down.

2. Continue with cadmium yellow to paint the shape of the strip of water left by the ebbing tide. Thin the wash in places with clear water.

3. Wet the top sections again if they have dried, and paint in cadmium red, wet in wet.

4. Add streaks of the same red near the horizon and soften with a clean brush.

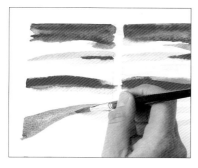

5. Continue the red lower down to create the shape of the sand bank.

6. Add yellow horizontal streaks in the water area.

7. Work on the foreground sand area in orange and add a red streak to the water. Paint red wet in wet over the sand area.

8. Add red to the far sand bank and to the yellow streaks in the sky to add depth.

9. Paint a thin wash of burnt umber at the top of the sky.

10. Use a thicker burnt umber mix to paint the town's silhouette in the distance.

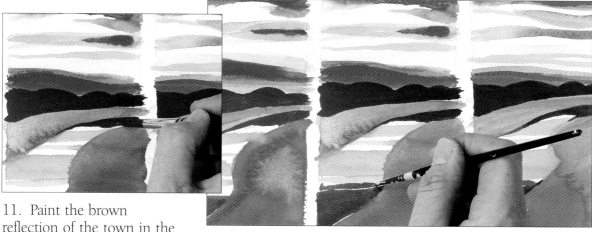

11. Paint the brown reflection of the town in the water, using burnt umber.

12. Use the same brush full of burnt umber to paint over the red area in the foreground of the water. Paint a streak of red above it to reflect the sunset.

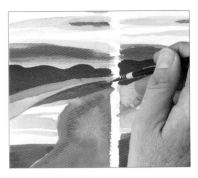

13. Paint red under the brown curve in the water, and soften the edges of the brown area.

14. Paint more yellow over the now dry red of the sky to soften it. Soften the lower edge of the town area with clear water to create shadow.

15. Using a rigger brush and red mixed with brown, paint the textured area on the near sand bank. Add more texture in red, making the marks larger towards the foreground.

16. Paint the buildings of the town and use the rigger brush to add masts, suggesting boats in the harbour. Then paint the reflections of the buildings.

17. Glaze red over the foreground sand bank. Add texture to the shadow of the town by taking out colour using clear water.

18. Cut out the best painting of the three using a craft knife, a cutting mat and a straight edge. Place it on folded white card and draw an outline for the background card using a straight edge and judging the width of the border by eye.

19. Cut out the background card, squeeze all-purpose glue on to the back of the painting, ½cm (¼in) from each edge. Mount it on the background card.

*The finished painting looks fresh and immediate and is not
bogged down by unnecessary detail. The dark silhouette of the
town makes the sunset really glow in contrast.*

The seascapes can be imaginary or inspired by a holiday postcard or photograph. Start with the sky, find the horizon and stick to three simple elements such as sky, sea and rocks or sky, sea and palms. Reflections of the sky in water, ripples caused by the wind or tide, eddies, waves or surf are all built up gradually using glazes painted on top of dried washes.

Chicken on the Run

I have a bird table in the garden and I had a loved budgie in a cage who lived to be eleven years old, a record I think! Birds are fascinating and one appealing image is of the brainless chicken dashing around, feathers flying, ridiculous and endlessly amusing. My large collection of feathers has been enlarged greatly by the feathers collected in friends' gardens: pretty, speckled bantam feathers, and long, green cockerel tail feathers.

You will need

Smooth satin watercolour paper, 12.5 x 18cm (5 x 7in) 300gsm (140lb)

Brushes: no. 6 round and rigger

Watercolours: cadmium yellow, cadmium red, yellow ochre and burnt umber

Tracing paper

Orange card, at least 380 x 140mm (15 x 5½in)

Large soft pencil, fine, hard pencil and putty eraser

Craft knife and cutting mat

Ruler or set square

Feathers

Toothbrush

Double-sided tape

All-purpose glue

1. Work over scrap paper. Trace the chicken using a soft pencil. Turn the tracing over and use the same pencil and a craft knife to scrape graphite over the traced lines.

2. Rub the graphite gently along the lines of the drawing with your finger.

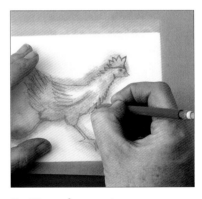

3. Turn the tracing over again and place it on your watercolour paper. Draw over the image with a fine, hard pencil to transfer it on to the paper.

4. Redraw the image using a fine pencil and removing any smudges with a putty eraser.

5. Take a no. 6 brush and a mix of cadmium yellow and yellow ochre, and paint around the pencil marks to outline the chicken image.

6. Wash in the middle of the chicken using a thin wash of cadmium yellow.

7. Paint the shadow of the chicken's wing using the darker mix. Use a clean, moist brush to lift out highlights from the wing, giving the chicken form.

8. Use cadmium red to paint the legs, feet, crest and beak.

9. Use burnt umber to pick out the shadows on the chicken's crest, the eye and the outline of the beak.

10. Use a rigger brush and some burnt umber added to the yellowy colour to accentuate the chicken's feathery outline. Add dark brown tones to the legs and feet using burnt umber.

11. Use yellow ochre and cadmium yellow to wash pale streaks on to the ground. Add brown streaks mixed from burnt umber and yellow ochre for a straw-like texture. Allow to dry.

12. Dip a toothbrush in cadmium yellow, cadmium red and yellow ochre, without mixing the paints well. Pull back the bristles with your finger and spatter the paint over the chicken.

13. Use a craft knife to cut along the edge of the feathers on the chicken's wing.

14. Push feathers into the holes in the paper, and arrange them to look like the chicken's tail.

15. Apply double-sided tape to the back of the card to secure the feathers in place.

16. Trim the chicken painting so that the tail feathers overlap the top. Place it on orange card folded at the side, judging the width of the borders by eye. Using a craft knife and cutting mat, cut out the orange card. The front of my card measures 190 x 140mm (7½ x 5½in). Remove the backing from the double-sided tape. Apply all-purpose glue to back of the chicken painting and stick it to the card.

17. Draw a line around the orange card a little way from the chicken painting, using a pencil and a straight edge.

18. Paint over the pencil line using a rigger brush and burnt umber mixed with cadmium red.

This handsome chicken looks as though he is in a tearing hurry. The humour of the painting is in the movement caused by the brush strokes on the ground, the spatters and the chicken's racing legs.

The addition of the feathers gives some of these birds a comical look, and you can choose outrageous colours to complete the effect. The robin and goose pictures would make ideal Christmas cards. The goose shows how you can make a really effective card using only one colour and a simple image.

Dog Daisies

Flowers cover a multitude of occasions: birthdays, weddings, anniversaries; 'being bunched' as my mother used to call it, is a very great pleasure, and so is the painting of flowers. If I am sent flowers for some reason I always try to paint them before they fade so that I have a memory of them. Little flower paintings make perfect cards to send to people. You don't have to paint a whole bunch: a single bloom, a simple daisy or a flowering shrub in the garden will do.

For this painting you need watercolour paper with a little texture: I have used fine grain.

You will need

Pad of fine grain watercolour paper, 15 x 25cm (6 x 10in), 300gsm (140lb)

Watercolour paper for the card, 25 x 27.5cm (9 x 10¾in)

Brushes: no. 6 and no. 12 round

Watercolours: cadmium red, cadmium yellow, viridian, burnt umber, cerulean blue, yellow ochre

Tracing paper

Pencil

Masking fluid and an old paintbrush

Craft knife and cutting mat

Paper tissue

Gold metallic gel pen

1. Transfer your image on to the fine grain watercolour paper using tracing paper and a pencil (see page 22).

2. Use masking fluid and an old paintbrush to paint the flowers, stems and the outline of the vase. Wash the brush immediately after use.

3. Mix cadmium yellow with a touch of viridian and apply a pale, watery wash to the whole painting using a large no. 12 wash brush. Leave white areas for highlights in the glass vase.

4. Mix viridian with a touch of yellow ochre to brown it a little and drop it in wet in wet from the top of the painting.

5. Mix viridian with burnt umber to add darker areas around the flowers, then drop in a lighter mix of yellow and green on the right-hand side.

6. Take a paper tissue and fold it length ways to dab out paint where the lighter leaves will be.

7. Continue painting with the darker green round the vase. Paint cerulean blue over the yellow wash in the glass to create a cooler green.

8. Mix burnt umber with viridian to make a very dark green, and paint around the areas of the lighter leaves to create negative shapes.

9. Using the no. 6 brush and the dark green, paint the ragged dark leaf shape against the lighter background.

10. When the painting is completely dry, rub off the masking fluid, which will now be hard, with a very clean finger.

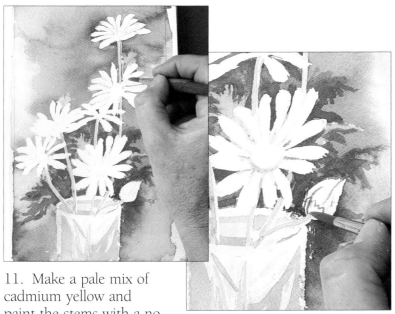

11. Make a pale mix of cadmium yellow and paint the stems with a no. 6 brush. Paint the details of the flowers with the same colour, creating definition around the petals and hearts.

12. Paint the green details of the little leaves round the bud with the same green.

13. Paint the hearts of the daisies with the cadmium yellow, leaving a little white paper in the middle as a highlight.

14. Mix cadmium red and cadmium yellow to paint the shadows under the flower hearts. Allow the painting to dry.

15. Trim the painting to 120 x 210cm (4¾ x 8¼in) and stick double-sided tape to the back. Fold the other sheet of watercolour paper lengthways for the card. Use pencil marks to help you place your painting on the front.

16. Use a ruler to help you draw pencil marks from the corners of the paintings to the corners of the card. Use these marks as a guide to draw a line border in gold metallic gel pen.

This painting of dog daisies really shows off the wet in wet technique which
makes a wonderful background for flower paintings. The use of the masking
fluid means that the flowers keep their petals pristine white against the green.

These flower paintings all show the wet in wet technique used to good effect in their backgrounds. For the morning glory, yucca cactus and the lilies I used the wax resist technique to delineate the shapes of the leaves.

Black Cat

Animal subjects are all around us. A friend of mine has forty-five assorted fowl and two donkeys! I have two cats and draw them all the time. This little black cat is made up and the black is created from three other colours mixed together. The simplicity of the shape with the shine down the back seems very expressive to me and the little stick-on yellow butterflies give the card and the cat a focus.

1. Trace the design and turn the tracing over. Use a craft knife to scrape graphite from a pencil over the back of the pencil lines.

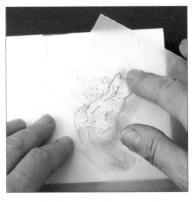

2. Rub the graphite with your finger along the lines of the drawing.

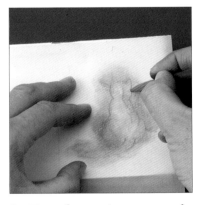

3. Turn the tracing over and place the cat design in position on the paper. Use a fine pencil to go over the lines of the design.

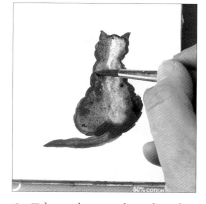

4. Mix a black wash from burnt umber, Prussian blue and alizarin crimson and using a no. 2 brush, 'draw' the outline of the cat.

5. Paint down the side of the cat, making the edge darker than the middle to create form.

6. Take a damp, clean brush and lift out paint to create a highlight down the cat's back and tail.

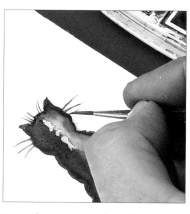

7. Take a rigger brush and paint whiskers, starting near the cheek and slowly lifting the brush to make fine points at the ends.

8. Make a cadmium lemon wash and paint in the grass with a no. 6 brush.

9. Add a small touch of viridian to the wet yellow wash for shadow.

10. Draw butterfly shapes on to the sticky end (though not the sticky side) of a self-adhesive memo note.

11. Cut out the butterflies using nail scissors, stick them to the card adding a dot of glue if necessary. Remove pencil marks with a putty eraser.

12. Paint details on the butterflies using yellow ochre and a fine no. 2 brush.

13. Add little dashes of the same colour to the grass to create texture, and leave the painting to dry.

14. Use a set square and a craft knife on a cutting mat to trim the painting.

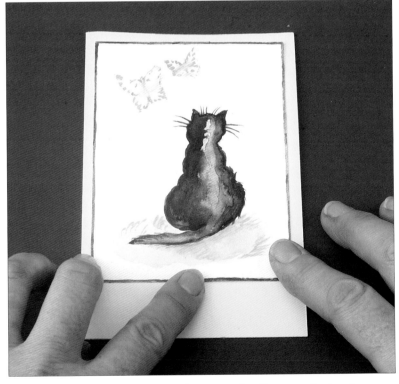

15. Mix a little viridian with the black colour you used for the cat and paint a fine line round the edge of the trimmed painting using a rigger brush.

16. Take a scored and folded piece of yellow card. Apply double-sided tape to the back of the painting and place it on the card, leaving twice as much border at the bottom as at the top and sides.

*The pale yellow fluttering butterflies make a little shadow
on the paper which give the card an extra dimension.
Painting an animal from behind cuts out the complication
of detail if your drawing skills are not up to scratch!*

All these animal cards have little decorative elements stuck on to add to the fun, except for the snails. These were cut out and stuck on to the background with 3D foam squares, and would be ideal for a 'Sorry I was late' card. The pig has ears and a tail made from the same paper and stuck on to provide humour and movement. The mother and baby rabbits would be good to send to a child who has a new brother or sister.

41

Lemons on Blue

A still life is a useful subject to paint as domestic objects sitting around the house can easily be arranged into a pretty composition, and then with an unusual way of framing or mounting they can be jazzed up to look fresh and original. When I had painted these lemons, I though they looked a little boring so I made up a table cloth by tracing a patterned scarf. The wavy lined border is where I ran out of pattern!

You will need

Smooth watercolour block, 250gsm (90lb)

No. 6 round brush

Cadmium yellow, lemon yellow, yellow ochre, Prussian blue, ultramarine blue, alizarin crimson

Dark blue card, 286 x 205mm (11¼ x 8in)

Pencil and putty eraser

White candle

White gouache

Paper tissue

Tracing paper

Craft knife and cutting mat

Spray mount

1. Arrange three lemons as shown and sketch them from life. Take a candle and 'draw' highlights with it on the lemon drawings.

2. Painting from life, wash lemon yellow over the whole area of the lemons. The highlights will remain white because of the wax resist from the candle.

3. Mix yellow ochre with a tiny bit of Prussian blue to paint the shadowed areas.

4. Mix a little Prussian blue and lemon yellow to make green and paint this around the mound at the end of the foreground lemon.

5. When the painting is dry, add details using cadmium yellow mixed with yellow ochre and ultramarine blue. Allow to dry again.

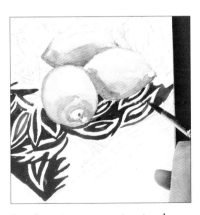

6. Trace the fabric pattern and transfer it on to the painting as shown on page 22, leaving a gap for the lemons.

7. Mix ultramarine blue and alizarin crimson and begin to paint the fabric pattern using a no. 6 brush.

8. Continue to paint in the pattern, turning the paper around as you go so that you don't smudge your work. Load the brush with paint and let it sit on the paper.

43

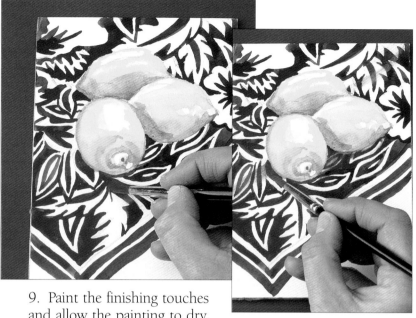

9. Paint the finishing touches and allow the painting to dry.

10. When the painting is dry, take a brush wet with clear water and sweep it across the patterned area around the lemons to suggest shadows from gentle creases in the fabric.

11. Blot the wetted paint with paper tissue to suggest highlights.

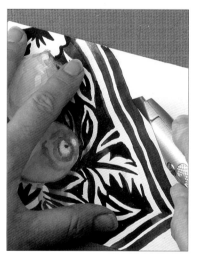

12. Remove the pencil lines from around the point at the bottom of the fabric with a putty eraser. Using a craft knife and a cutting mat, cut around the point.

13. Turn the painting over and apply spray mount lightly to the back. Always work in a well-ventilated room when using spray mount.

14. Take your sheet of dark blue card and score and fold it in half. Stick the painting to the front of the card. Paint a white line all the way round, just beyond the edge of the painting, using white gouache.

The purply blue background is complementary to
the yellow lemons, making a pleasing combination
for a really striking card. The asymmetric framing
takes the design out of the ordinary.

Introducing patterns can enliven still life subjects. You can also achieve this by cutting a composition in two and using only half of it – dare to be different! The sculptural quality of shells, and their subtle, natural colours make them fascinating to paint.

Index